T0018339

EYES, NOSE, BELLY, TOES

EYES, NOSE, BELLY, TOES

My First Human Body Book

Krupa Bhojani Playforth, MD ● Illustrations by **Becky Paige**

callisto
publishing
an imprint of Sourcebooks

**To my kids and to my patients,
who are constant reminders of the wonder
and the resilience of the human body.**

Copyright © 2024 by Callisto Publishing LLC
Cover and internal design © 2024 by Callisto Publishing LLC
Illustrations by Becky Paige.
Author photo courtesy of Jamie Sutera Photography.

Art Director: Angela Navarra
Art Producer: Stacey Stambaugh
Editor: Adrian Potts
Outline Editor: Kristen Depken
Production Editor: Rachel Taenzler
Production Manager: Martin Worthington

Callisto Kids and the colophon are registered trademarks of Callisto Publishing LLC.

All rights reserved. No part of this book may be reproduced in any form or by any electronic or mechanical means including information storage and retrieval systems—except in the case of brief quotations embodied in critical articles or reviews—without permission in writing from its publisher, Sourcebooks LLC.

Published by Callisto Publishing LLC C/O Sourcebooks LLC
P.O. Box 4410, Naperville, Illinois 60567-4410
(630) 961-3900
callistopublishing.com

This product conforms to all applicable CPSC and CPSIA standards.

Source of Production: 1010 Printing Asia Limited, Kwun Tong, Hong Kong, China
Date of Production: July 2023
Run Number: SBCAL98

Printed and bound in China.
OGP 10 9 8 7 6 5 4 3 2 1

Introduction

Children have an innate curiosity about their bodies. Research shows that even young infants make observations about the world around them and can quickly learn how to physically engage with their environments. As children mature and become increasingly aware of all that their bodies can do, that curiosity deepens.

This book offers a developmentally layered approach to teach your toddler about their body. As a pediatrician and a mother, I wanted to write a book that can be read multiple times to the same child at different phases of their development.

Read this book with young toddlers and focus on labeling body parts, which is an important language milestone. Model pointing at their body parts, or yours, as you name each one.

As your toddler gets older, layer that knowledge with information about how different parts of the body work together and how they physically interact with the world. Try practicing some fine motor skills (like holding an object or clapping) and gross motor skills (such as bending the limbs or jumping) listed in the book. Show your child how those body parts work in tandem; for example, how the knee, leg, and foot work together to kick a ball.

And finally, for all toddlers, my hope is this book can reinforce the message that the world is diverse. Regardless of how different we all look on the surface, we are all people and each one of us is important.

Every **body** is special
in any size, color, or shape.

Bodies have lots of parts,
and each part has a big job to do!

This is the **head**.
Can you point to yours?

The head has many parts:
hair, eyes, ears, nose, and mouth.

Hair grows on your head.

It can be curly or straight, short or long;
brown, red, blond, or black.

You have two **eyes** that help you see.

They make tears
when you cry

and close when you sleep.

On each side of your head are your **ears**.

They help you
listen to music, songs,
and stories.

This is your **nose**! You use it to smell.
Some smells are nice, like apple pie and flowers.

Some smells are stinky,
like old socks and skunks.

When you feel happy, you smile with your **mouth**.

You eat with your mouth
and talk, laugh, play music, and sing!

Your **neck** holds your head
and can move it around.
You can look up at the sky
or low at the ground.

Next are your **shoulders**. You have a pair.
They can go up to your ears,

or move down and around.

Your **arms** have parts that
all work together.
You use them to reach, climb,
carry, and hug.

Here is the **elbow**! Can you find yours?

It straightens and bends.
Try to pick up, throw, and catch a ball.

This is a **hand**.
It can hold crayons and draw.

With two hands, you can clap.
Find a friend and high-five!

There are ten **fingers** on your hands for pointing and wiggling.

1 2 3 4 5

Use them for tickling and counting!

Under your shirt is your **belly**.
The belly button is in the middle.
When you eat, food goes into your belly.

This is your **back**. It helps move your head, neck, shoulders, arms, and legs.

It can twist, stretch,
and let you bend down.

Your body has two **legs**.
They are so strong!
Your legs hold the body up
to stand or to walk.

These are your **knees**,
where the legs bend.

Bend your knees to jump.
Or, ride a bike at the playground.

The **ankles** connect your
legs to your feet.
They let feet move up and down
and side to side.

Look at the ends of your legs to find your **feet**. They can be very ticklish!

Use your feet to kick,
run, and stomp.

There are ten **toes** on your feet.

Your toes can wiggle and stretch!

Now you know all about your **body** and the amazing things it can do.

From your eyes to your nose,
to your belly and your toes!

About the Author

 **Krupa Bhojani Playforth, MD**, is a board-certified pediatrician and a mother of three who believes every parent deserves clear, nuanced answers to their child health questions. She grew up in Malawi and now lives in Northern Virginia with her family. Dr. Playforth is the founder of The Pediatrician Mom, a website where parents can find evidence-based, practical answers for all their child health questions. She loves to write, read fantasy novels, and attempt to impose order on her chaotic life (unsuccessfully). You can learn more about Dr. Playforth at ThePediatricianMom.com.

About the Illustrator

 **Becky Paige** is an illustrator living in sunny Orlando, Florida. She loves creating images that are sweet, colorful, and playful. After years as a classroom teacher, she had the opportunity to study graphic design and follow her lifelong dream of being an illustrator. In her spare time, she enjoys watching movies, going on walks, drawing, and spending time with her family.